My Dream Is You

I can't say I love you enough
because it is the most
beautiful, complete feeling
    I have ever had
    Over and over again
    I love you

— Susan Polis Schutz

My Dream Is You

A collection of poems on love
Edited by Susan Polis Schutz

Blue Mountain Press ™

Boulder, Colorado

Library of Congress Catalog Card Number: 87-72258
ISBN: 0-88396-259-4

The following works have previously appeared in Blue Mountain Arts publications:

"Thank You for the Day We Met" and "I Want Our Relationship to Last," by Susan
Polis Schutz. Copyright © Stephen Schutz and Susan Polis Schutz, 1986. "I can't say I
love you enough," by Susan Polis Schutz. Copyright © Stephen Schutz and Susan
Polis Schutz, 1987. "I Will Always Love You," by Pamela J. Owens Renfro; "I Like You,
I Love You," by Collin McCarty; and "All I ever need is you," by Shelly Roberts.
Copyright © Blue Mountain Arts, Inc., 1985. "Our love is stronger . . . ," by Deanne
Laura Kennedy; "I Will Always Care About You," by Irene Roberts; "As Time Goes
By," by Joan M. Klinko; "You and I fell in love," by Edmund O'Neill; "I Have Learned
with You," by Rhonda Lynn Simmons; and "You're the Best There Is," "Forever,"
"What I Want to Be to You," "We Are So Good Together," and "Please
understand . . . ," by Collin McCarty. Copyright © Blue Mountain Arts, Inc., 1986. "My
Dream Is You," by Robin Wrightmore; "Thank You for Loving Me," by Linda Olson;
"You Will Always Have My Love," by Patti Packard; "Every Day, I Realize More and
More," by Mary Shafer; "You Are Everything I Ever Dreamed Love Could Be," by
Donna Levine; "You're My Favorite Way to Spend My Time," by Diana M.
Beauchemin; "Did I Ever Say Thanks," by Carey Martin; "When two people fall
in love . . . ," by Tracey Kuharski; and "When I Say 'I Love You' . . . ,"
by Arletha Miles. Copyright © Blue Mountain Arts, Inc., 1987. All rights reserved.

Thanks to the Blue Mountain Arts creative staff.

ACKNOWLEDGMENTS appear on page 62.

Manufactured in the United States of America
First printing: October, 1987

Blue Mountain Press INC.

P.O. Box 4549, Boulder, Colorado 80306

CONTENTS

My Dream Is You

Once, I was afraid I'd never
    find someone
to really care about.
I wanted someone perfect,
at least for me.

A special kind of talking, an honest
    way of listening;
    not being afraid to laugh or cry;
    kindness and understanding;
    fun and excitement;
    someone who would lift my heart
    with joy.

I guess I expected a lot,
    but I'm a believer!
    And I believed that someday
    someone's particular magic
        would transform my life.

So, in spite of all the waiting,
    all the loneliness,
    all the almost-giving-up,
    it's been worth it;
    it's all been worthwhile.
And wishes really do come true,
    because what I always wanted
    isn't a dream —

    it's you.

— Robin Wrightmore

When you first came into my life . . .

I had no idea how easy you would be to talk to,
and I never imagined that our early conversations
would grow into such a strong friendship.
I never suspected that we'd discover
so many common interests and values,
or that I could ever enjoy simple pleasures
    as much as when they are shared with you.

I never thought we'd have so many
warm and happy times together,
or that your compassion would help so much
    to ease me through the rougher times.

I didn't expect to feel so soon
as though I'd known you forever,
or to trust you so easily
    with my secrets and deepest feelings.

I never thought your support could make
    such a difference,
that your encouragement
would bring my dreams closer,
make my successes sweeter
and my losses easier to accept.

I never imagined that I would grow
to want,
to need,
and to love you so much.

When you first came into my life,
I never dreamed you'd soon be someone
    whom I couldn't live without.

— Paula Finn

Thank You for the Day We Met
and I Love You

Ever since the day we met
I knew that you were extremely special
I knew that I wanted to get to
   know you better
and I knew that my emotions
   had been touched
Ever since the day I fell in love with you
I knew that I wanted to spend all my time
   with you
I knew that I wanted to tell you everything
   about myself
I knew that I would begin to grow
   as a person
Ever since the day that you and I became one
I knew that we had a very
   poignant relationship
I knew that my body and mind
   were passionate forever
I knew that I wanted our relationship
   to last forever
If we had not met
I would still be searching for happiness
and I would always be thinking that
   love was not real
So I want to dearly thank you
for the day we met and forever after
I love you

— Susan Polis Schutz

Our love is stronger because of all
that we've been through together...

Relationships are never easy,
  and you and I have had our share
of struggling and troubled times,
but together we made it.
Together, we cared enough to
  face our problems — we loved enough
not to let go.
And now, what we have is even stronger
  because of all we've been through,
    all we struggled with.
I sometimes worry about the future,
but with you by my side
the future seems much brighter —
the present more precious, more
    meaningful.
We need the tears to appreciate the
    laughter,

we must share our problems to realize
    how much we truly need each other —
to give our love the chance to expand,
    to strengthen, to endure.
We deserve nothing less than a love
    that will remain through all aspects
    of our lives.
Together, we will face all obstacles
    with confidence,
because we already know our relationship
    can endure even the worst of times,
as long as we love — share —
    and stay together.

                            — Deanne Laura Kennedy

I Will Always Care About You

I sometimes think you really don't know
   how very important you are to me.
You have put new meaning and awareness
   into my life.
I know closeness when we are together.
I really care about you;
it's important to me that you are safe,
and important to me that you are well.
I feel a sense of loss when we're apart;
sometimes I wonder if we could not have
   more time together.
Then I think about the comfort of your
   arms around me —
that keeps me going for a while —
and I know that soon we'll be together.
Your touch will make all things right
   in my world —
it always does.
Wherever our decisions may take us —
   I will always care about you,
   I will always remember,
   there will always be a place for you
      in my heart.

— Irene Roberts

Thank You for Loving Me

Thank you for every thought, act, and word of love, even when I may not have deserved it.

Thank you for the time out of your life, when you could have spent it elsewhere.

Thank you for the confidence, when I was insecure and full of doubt.

Thank you for never disappointing me, even when your life would have been easier if you had.

Thank you for making me feel and know I was the most beautiful person in the world, at times when I didn't feel it.

Thank you for sharing the hard times in my life, even when yours may have been harder and your responsibilities greater.

Thank you for loving me, even enough at times to let me go my own way.

And thank you for letting me return to you, and for letting me know that I was always meant to be yours.

— Linda Olson

You Will Always Have My Love

Sometimes I wonder what it is that I did
    to deserve you . . .
the love and happiness I am feeling,
the countless smiles you have brought
    to my face,
the sheer joy you have given my life
    since you have entered it.
My days are brightened just by hearing
    your voice;
my nights, by having you next to me;
and every minute in between,
by knowing that you are there,
    even when you are miles away.
I will hold you in my heart —
cradle you in the depths of my soul —
    for as long as you wish to be there.
You have shown me your friendship,
    your love, your understanding,
        and your trust.
And sometimes I wonder what I could
    ever do to repay you.
Then I realize that all you really
    want from me is my love . . .
and that, you know, you already have.

— Patti Packard

Every Day, I Realize More and More
How Much I Love You

Every day, I realize more and more
    how very much I love you
and how much it means to me to know
that you are there for me to share
    in all the moments of my life.

There are times when I have to keep
    my focus on you and me,
when I have to look ahead and not worry,
but I trust you with my heart
    and my love.
I believe in our hopes and dreams,
and that the love we have for each other
    is enough to weather the storms
        that come our way.

I know we can only live and love
    one day at a time,
but how very comforting to know
    that you want to share your days
        with me.

My greatest happiness lies in the
    intertwining of our dreams,
        hopes, hearts, and minds.

With all my heart, I love you.

— Mary Shafer

I Love You
with All that I Am

I could never tell you
how much I love you
My feelings for you are something
that cannot be measured
for they have no beginning or end
Trying to explain the depth and
complexity of what I feel for you
is as impossible as trying
to completely explain the intricacies
  of my soul
I love you
  with all that I have
    with all that I do
      with all that I dream
        with all that I am.

Somewhere deep inside me
beyond the level that I can comprehend
  and understand
my every thought
my every word
and my every deed
are motivated by my love for you.

—Garry LaFollette

You Are Everything I Ever Dreamed Love Could Be

You are my love.
You are the person who holds me
    when I need to be held.
You are the person I share my
    everyday thoughts and concerns with,
the one who understands and comforts me.
You are my bright tomorrow.

I want to be all of these things for you.
I want to be able to give you all the
    love you need,
and also the time you need to develop
    your own interests
and reach your own goals.

We have made a commitment
to love and respect one another,
and I want you to know
    that my commitment to you is still
        strong and true,
    my love for you is still growing deeper,
    and my most heartfelt wish is for you
        to have the best that life
            can offer, always.

— Donna Levine

I Like You, I Love You

I know this is sort of
a funny thing to say, but
   I'll say it anyway . . .
      I like liking you.
It makes me feel good to
be alive and in this world with you.

So much happiness comes
from your gentle ways
and from our together days.
Right from the very beginning
I realized your importance to me . . .
   I like the way your eyes smile at me,
      the way we touch,
         the way we laugh,
            the way we are.
I like having dreams we both
   want to reach out for.
I like knowing that we only get closer
   as the time goes by.

And I want you to know
   that in addition
to all the wonderful things
   I like, it's also true
      that I love . . .
         loving you.

— Collin McCarty

All I ever need is you
to kiss away the tears
and wipe away my frowns.
All I ever need is your love
to help me through lonely nights
and to make me smile
after a long day.
All I ever need is to hear
    you whisper softly
        "I love you"
        when I wake in
            the morning
and before I fall asleep
        at night
    to make my life
        fully complete.

— Shelly Roberts

As Time Goes By,
Our Love Will Only Grow Deeper

I love you.
I can't say it enough to show how happy
    I've become.
There is a strong feeling in my heart
    that gives me self-confidence.
I am a better person because I not only
have faith in myself, but also the faith
you have given me from your love,
    your trust.
I love you.
There is a certain bond between us,
expressed by touch and by that part
of life we have experienced together.
This is serious love, not infatuation,
a love I hope will last forever, so that
as time continues, we can only
    be drawn closer.
I love you.
I have finally learned what it means.
It's a feeling that only comes with experience.
And I can't say it enough.
I love you.

— Joan M. Klinko

You're the Best There Is

The best times of my life
   are the times I spend with you.
The more I know you, the more
I believe it's true . . .
   that you're the best there is.

The best memories are made with you.
The best days are spent with you.
The best feelings are felt with you.
The best sentiments are saved for you.
The best love is made with you.
The best thoughts, the best dreams,
   the best life I could ever have . . .
      come only to me through you.

For to me, you truly are the best there is.

— Collin McCarty

I Want Our Relationship to Last

I thought I would never
find the right person to love
until I met you
And since I have
always thought that
love is the most
important part of my life
I want our love to last and
to be as beautiful
as it is now
I want our love
to be the backbone
of our lives forever

Our love came naturally
but I know that
we must both work
at making it last
so I will try my hardest
at all times
to be fair and honest with you
I will strive for my own goals
and help you achieve yours

I will always try
to understand you
I will always
let you know what I am thinking
I will always
try to support you
I will try
to successfully blend
our lives together
with enough freedom
to grow as individuals
I will always
consider each day
with you special
Regardless of
what events
occur in our lives
I will make
sure that our
relationship flourishes
as I will always
love and respect
you

— Susan Polis Schutz

I Give You My Life in Love for Always

If I shared every thought about you
   that came to mind,
there would never be enough time
   to hold them.
If I told you how much I love you,
   words would be inadequate
to express how I feel.
If I held you forever,
   it would seem like only a moment,
because there would never be
   enough time to share my love with you.
If I spent every day with you
   from now until forever,
it would never be long enough,
because our love holds more than
   a lifetime to share.
Even so, I give you all my tomorrows
   today,
and I give you my life
   in love
from now, for always.

— Carolyn Flinn McCool

I Love You for
All You Are to Me

From the day we met,
you have shown me
   the best in life.
You have been the one
who introduced me
   to new experiences,
      exciting places,
         warm love.
You were the one
who taught me how
to be together with someone,
how to enjoy every day
for what it is,
and how to see good
in everything.

You were the one
who showed me
just how much love
I have inside,
and you were the one
who released that love
    and sent it soaring.
You, my one and only love,
showered me with warmth
    and affection.
You love me,
    and I love you.

— Pamela J. Owens Renfro

I Have More Reasons
than Ever to Love You

You didn't notice,
but I was looking at you
    the other day.
I was thinking about
  how much time
    has passed around us.
The outside world
exerts so much pressure,
and just living from day to day
    has a tendency
to make us forget those things
that are important to us,
such as what first
    brought us together.
    That's why I just had to stop
      for that moment,
and look at you,
to see and recall all those reasons
    I fell in love with you
in the first place.
And you know what?
Not only did I recall them all;
I found so many new reasons
to love you even more.

— Denys Lesiw, Jr.

When two people fall in love . . .

When two people fall in love,
they share equally with each other.
They become one.
A bond is built, along with trust
    and loyalty.
They accept each other for what they are.
They love each other for who they are.
They are there for each other
    to comfort when they are down.
When one hurts, the other hurts.
They communicate with each other.
The problems they have are worked out.
They work on their relationship together.

They learn to grow with each other.
They accept challenges as they come.
Sometimes they are scared,
    but they are always there for one another.
They are one,
but they have their own minds,
their own ideas, and different ways
    of thinking.
They love and learn, cry and feel.
They are there to help each other.
They are not perfect; they make mistakes.
Their lives are lived happily,
when two people fall in love.

— Tracey Kuharski

You and I fell in love
so soon after we first met,
and I believed then that
the feelings my heart held for you
could never be deeper or stronger
than in that first excitement
of discovering our special love.
But now, the more we're together,
I come to realize that our love
encompasses so much more
than those first emotions.
For each idea and feeling,
spoken freely and in trust, increases
our understanding of each other.
Each moment we share,
smiling or in tears, brings us
another memory for our future.
Each challenge or dream we meet,
together or individually, offers us
the opportunity to grow
    and strengthen our lives.

And all these things,
together with all our potentials,
have deepened the love
we felt from the first moment.
You have helped me to grow
in ways I've never known,
and all those new spaces within me
are so full of love for you.

— Edmund O'Neill

I Love You

I love your mind
for in it I have found the core
   of your being.
It is the well from which spring
   forth your wisdom, compassion,
      intelligence, and life.

I love your face
   for in it I see the sunshine of
      tomorrow.
It is the mirror that reflects the
   goodness of your heart.

I love your arms
   for in them I find the strength and
      security I so desperately need.
They are the life line to my peace
   of mind,
      the cable to which I cling.

I love your hands
   for in them I find the talent and
      sensitivity that bring out my
         respect and admiration.
Your touch so gentle,
   your caress so sweet.

I love your body
　　for in it I find the desire and
　　　　warmth that make me fulfilled.
It is precious and priceless —
　　the outward representation of your
　　　　inward beauty.

I love you
　　for you are the embodiment,
　　　　the personification, of all that
　　　　　　I seek.
You are my joy for today,
　　my hope for tomorrow.

In you, I have found myself,
　　my life,
　　　　my love.

— Karen Hosey

Forever

How can you ever explain
   some of the deepest feelings
      you've ever felt for someone?

You try to tell them with words
   that speak of joy and gratitude
         and so much love;
You try to show them with touches,
   with smiles chasing away the tears,
   with little caresses that say you care,
   with secret intimacies you share.

You make the most of each day together;
You take the time to make your love
   the best it can possibly be.
You do whatever you can
   and whatever it takes, and you hope
   that their heart understands
      what your heart is trying to say
      when it says . . .
"I love you,
   and I know
      I'll always feel that way."

— Collin McCarty

You're My Favorite Way
to Spend My Time

I can't stop thinking of you,
   and when I'm thinking of you,
I can't stop smiling.

I want to be with you,
   because when I'm with you,
I feel wonderful.

I like to hold you,
   because when I'm holding you,
I'm secure.

I enjoy talking with you,
   for when I'm talking with you,
I'm being honest.

I want to share with you,
   because sharing with you
allows me to give myself to you.

Because of you,
smiling,
feeling wonderful,
being secure and honest,
and giving to you,
are my most favorite ways
   to spend my time.

— Diana M. Beauchemin

I Can't Imagine My Life
Without You

When we are together,
it feels so right.
I am at peace with myself,
and the problems of the day
don't seem so large
or so important.

When we have a disagreement,
the hurt won't go away
until we can share our feelings
and find a way to compromise
and make it right between us.

I can't imagine my life
    without you,
or imagine how it was
before we met.
I love you so much.

— Boots Thompson

We Have Found Love

You have touched a part
deep inside of me,
and now you are a tender warmth
that shares my innermost thoughts,
feelings, and dreams.
We have reached a special place
where few ever go,
for we have unlocked the doors
of trust and understanding.
Now we have found love,
and all the love we have found
is ours to laugh in, cry in,
even be silent in,
for it is all ours to share.
In you, I've found a place
so full of joy and love.
You have been hurt by love before,
but I will never hurt you;
I just want to enjoy
the love that is ours to take,
ours to give,
ours to share.
Now is a time to share;
it is a time for you and I
to enjoy
and to love
together.

— Rosielind Alcorn

I Have Learned with You
What Real Love Is

The day we met, something inside me
changed. I don't quite understand
it, but I do know the change is
because of you. It's such a good
feeling that I hope it never ends.
You're so different, and so unique,
compared to all the others in my life.
What a change you have made . . . It's as
if your soul has reached out and touched
mine. I feel magic inside like I've
never felt before. When you first
spoke, I listened intently so that I
could remember every word you said . . .
When you held my hand, your touch
was so gentle that I wouldn't have
known it was there if I hadn't felt
your sincerity.

When you're with me, I feel so warm
inside that I sometimes think I can feel
you holding me, when all you're doing
is looking into my eyes. The security
that I feel when you're around makes
me think that I have nothing to fear.
I can be with you all day, and when
we say good-bye, I do nothing but look
forward to the next time we're together . . .
My favorite things to do are to think
of you, dream of you, and count the
time until we're together again. No
one in my life has ever made me feel
the way you can make me feel. I have
learned with you what real love is.

— Rhonda Lynn Simmons

What I Want to Be to You

Your nicest memory of yesterday.
Your sweetest wish for tomorrow.
Your friend.
Your confidant.
Someone who makes you laugh.
Someone you know you can trust.
Someone you look for in your dreams.
The best lover you've ever known.
The knowledge that you'll never be alone.
Your companion on peaceful walks.
Your hand-holder and smile-sharer.
Someone who will always care.
Someone who will always be there.
Open arms and an open door,
    wanting always to be "home" to you.

— Collin McCarty

I Love You More than
Words Can Say

It isn't easy to find someone
 you really like
who likes you in return,
who isn't afraid to accept
 what you have to give
and give what you need.
It isn't easy,
 but I found you.

It takes a while to get to know
 someone well enough
to know that they can be trusted
 to respect your deepest feelings
and share their own secret dreams.
It takes a while,
 but you've made the time pass quickly.

It takes a special person
to love another for who they really are
and not for who they are imagined to be.
You are that person.

And I love you more than words can say.

— Stanfield Major II

You Are My Life

You are the sun that chases away
   my clouds,
the star that guides me through
   my uncertainties,
and the loving anchor in all my storms . . .

You are strength to my weakness,
belief to my doubts,
and the fulfillment of my
   most cherished dreams . . .

You are the comfort of my yesterdays,
the magic of my todays,
and the hope of my tomorrows . . .

You are the joy of my heart,
the peace of my soul,
and the love of my life . . .

My love,
   you are my life.

— Paula Finn

We Are So Good Together

We've got a good relationship . . .
and I really think that
    we will have a great one.
It will take a little effort
    —on both our parts—
but every single thing we learn in the process
about communication; about each other;
about our hopes for the future
    and our personal dreams;
about touching; about sharing;
about spending time and giving space;
about putting our energies into
    a good and rewarding place . . .
all these things will help us
    and not hurt us in any way.
I want us to grow and reach out
    for dreams . . . together.
And moving ahead doesn't mean
    having to leave anything behind.
It just means taking something
    —our relationship—and building
    upward and outward from the strength
       that is already there.

I love you, and I hope you'll always love me.
    With you is the place
       that I want to always stay,
         being as good together
            as we can possibly be.

— Collin McCarty

I Will Always Love You

I love you now
   for who you are now
I will love you tomorrow
   for who you will be then
And if you stay the same
   throughout the years
my love for you will not diminish
The excitement I feel with you
   will never fade
You will be as special to me
   tomorrow as you are today
And if you should change in any way
   my love for you will remain the same
I will not stop loving you.

— Pamela J. Owens Renfro

Did I Ever Say Thanks
for Loving Me?

Did I ever tell you
that if I had it to do
  all over again . . .
you would still be
  the only one
    I would ever want
      to share my life with?

Did I ever tell you
  how happy you make me
    feel inside?

If I never did . . .
    let me say these things
      to you now . . .

And remember the words forever,
  for that is as long
    as the feelings will last.

— Carey Martin

Please understand . . .

There is something
I would like you to know about me.
And about my feelings
    concerning you.

It's that I don't think I've ever been
so happy . . . or so afraid
    in all my life.
I'm scared because of what
I've gone through before with love;
I feel like it's taken me
a long time to pick up the pieces
of my life and put them back
together again.

Just when
I started feeling comfortable with
    life, in a lonely sort of way,
    you came along . . .
and now I know that
    there is nothing I'd rather do
        than love . . .
            and be loved . . .
                by you.

Just don't ever go away, okay?
The only things I want to leave
    are my feelings of being afraid.
I want everything about you
        and our tomorrows together
            to stay.

— Collin McCarty

When I Say "I Love You"...

I say the words "I love you" so much
that I wonder sometimes if you take for
granted the feeling that is behind them.
I never want you to see them as just words
to begin or end a conversation.
"I love you" is just my way of saying
that you have touched a place in my heart
and made me come alive.

You have claimed a part of my heart that,
no matter what happens to us,
will always belong to you.
You taught me how to love.
You broke through all of my defenses
and comforted my fears.
You touched places in me I never knew I had
and made me feel things
        I never thought I'd feel.
You have all of the patience, care,
understanding, and concern needed
to build the kind of relationship we have.

So when I say "I love you,"
the words are not spoken out of habit.
It is my way of saying thank you for
being you and of returning some
of the joy you have given me.

— Arletha Miles

ACKNOWLEDGMENTS

We gratefully acknowledge the permission granted by the following authors to reprint their works.

Garry LaFollette for "I Love You with All that I Am." Copyright © Garry LaFollette, 1987. All rights reserved. Reprinted by permission.

Carolyn Flinn McCool for "I Give You My Life in Love for Always." Copyright © Carolyn Flinn McCool, 1987. All rights reserved. Reprinted by permission.

Pamela J. Owens Renfro for "I Love You for All You Are to Me." Copyright © Pamela J. Owens Renfro, 1987. All rights reserved. Reprinted by permission.

Denys Lesiw, Jr. for "I Have More Reasons than Ever to Love You." Copyright © Denys Lesiw, Jr., 1987. All rights reserved. Reprinted by permission.

Karen Hosey for "I Love You." Copyright © Karen Hosey, 1985. All rights reserved. Reprinted by permission.

Boots Thompson for "I Can't Imagine My Life Without You." Copyright © Boots Thompson, 1987. All rights reserved. Reprinted by permission.

Rosielind Alcorn for "We Have Found Love." Copyright © Rosielind Alcorn, 1987. All rights reserved. Reprinted by permission.

Paula Finn for "You Are My Life." Copyright © Paula Finn, 1986. And for "When you first came into my life . . ." Copyright © Paula Finn, 1987. All rights reserved. Reprinted by permission.

Stanfield Major II for "I Love You More than Words Can Say." Copyright © Stanfield Major II, 1987. All rights reserved. Reprinted by permission.

A careful effort has been made to trace the ownership of poems used in this anthology in order to obtain permission to reprint copyrighted materials and to give proper credit to the copyright owners.

If any error or omission has occurred, it is completely inadvertent, and we would like to make corrections in future editions provided that written notification is made to the publisher: BLUE MOUNTAIN PRESS, INC., P.O. Box 4549, Boulder, Colorado 80306.